# 140 Ways Coping with

# Depression

© ALYSE KING

Copyright

COPING – 140 Ways Coping with Depression

Alyse King cmitrainingservices@gmail.com

Cover Photo by Alyse King
Back Cover by Ayse King
Edited by I.A. Mohabier, MA

ISBN Library of Congress Cataloging-In-Publication Date
**ISBN-13:978-1492919544, ISBN-10:1492919543**

King, Alyse King 2014

First Edition

Printed in the United States of America

# DEDICATION

*To All Children for their outstanding and remarkable progress*

# Contents

*"Do not be afraid, for I am with you. Do not be anxious, for I am your God. I will fortify you, yes, I will help you. I will really hold on to you wit my right  hand of righteousness"~Isaiah 41:10, 13*

*"Do not be afraid, for I am with you. Do not be anxious, for I am your God. I will fortify you, yes, I will help you. I will really hold on to you wit my right  hand of righteousness"~Isaiah 41:10, 13*

# Preface

In today's difficult and challenging economic environment, many factors contribute to mental health issues. No one is able to predict who may succumb to mental illness.

Parents all over the world who care about their children's mental health will want to read this book. I was shocked when mental illnesses struck two of my four children. Soon after, I was struck too. While caring for my children, I was diagnosed as suffering with major depression and stress.

This is my journey of how I coped with my two children's struggles with schizophrenia, major depression and bipolar disorders.

This is truly a heartbreaking journey with battling impossible odds to help my son cope after one psychiatrist told me that my son may never recover or may have only one-third chance of recovery. Once I received that devastating prognosis, I devoted all my waking hours to caring for him. I refused to accept the diagnosis. I wanted to prove the doctor wrong. I worked tirelessly until I received successful results. Little

1

did I know that I was being prepared for another shocking realization.

Six short years later, one of my daughters became mentally ill.

Like any other illness, knowledge and early detection of schizophrenia, major depression and bipolar disorders is vitally important to prevent years of pain and hardships. Unfortunately, the symptoms during the early stages of mental illness were truly deceptive and confusing. They were unsuspecting and gradual, which made it impossible to detect them as the beginning signs of mental illness.

My agonizing experience shows the importance of learning and understanding early signs of mental illness. Many Americans recognize the illnesses only when these illnesses have slipped far from reality, such as having a horrible breakdown.

This book is a story for any family who confronts difficulties with mental illnesses or any American living with the economic realities of 21st Century America, who cannot cope with mental breakdown. It is an inspirational book of faith and hope, and the bravery of not giving up or giving out.

It is impossible to imagine a journey into a life with paranoid schizophrenia, major depression and bi-polar disorders. It is a journey happening to someone else's sons and daughters. It is a journey that is, at times, embarrassing to tell. It is a journey that is all too heart breaking. At times, I felt that death would have been more comforting than living with the struggles and heartbreaks of mental illnesses.

The mass confusions that came from these illnesses caused both my son and daughter further feelings of hopelessness and helplessness.

There were constant, **"Why Me's,"** and many, **"What-Ifs."** Happily, over time, as their health improved, they were able to ask **"Why not me?"** or **"Why not us?"**

For years, with the severity and the debilitation from these illnesses, there was a near zero chance that my son and daughter would lead normal lives again. Their inabilities to accomplish any of life's tasks caused them many distresses, resulting in further mental breakdown. They desperately needed to cope, as the fears of mental illnesses were greater than their coping abilities. It was a very weighty and challenging task, but I continued

3

without let up to find new and different ways to help them. Learning new ways to cope was an on-going process.

This is a book of assuring **hope,** and **never releasing that hope.** All the recommendations offered in this book helped my son and daughter on their difficult roads to recovery. They may also be helpful to you.

I am writing this book to inspire others that in the face of unfathomable challenges with mental illness, one can learn to cope because there is hope for recovery.

The passing years have brought me much knowledge, experience and wisdom. During the course of writing this book, I learned how much my son and daughter endured and the outstanding courage and strength they displayed in the face of their adversities.

## Introduction

The most agonizing moment of my life was when I heard the psychiatrist say two words, *"Paranoid Schizophrenia."* Seconds later, I heard three more words, *"May Never Recover."* I was completely shocked. I was nearly paralyzed because I was not expecting to hear anything like that. The prognosis was only one-third chance of recovery. My son was only 18 years old.

Six years later, my 16-year-old daughter was diagnosed as suffering with **"Bi-polar Disorder" with "Psychosis."** I was completely heart-broken, devastated and for years I could not cope with the fact that my son and daughter may never recover.

This book tells about my journey to cope against impossible odds while struggling to help my son and daughter learn to manage and cope with their illnesses.

This book provides an overview of how I coped with my son's and daughter's mental illnesses. This is a compelling story of sheer determination and not giving up or giving in to the demands of mental illnesses. It tells about searching and finding new ways for me to cope as their mother

5

and caregiver and to provide them with the necessary coping skills.

This story has inspired many who are undergoing severe stresses and depression, someone who is caring for loved ones, or someone who may be losing hope that in the face of unfathomable challenges, there is hope for effectively coping with your loved one's illnesses.

This book is for readers looking for positive, uplifting, success stories of mothers who are single-handedly caring for their mentally ill sons and daughters and may feel hopeless because they cannot cope.

I chose to write this book to encourage parents who are struggling to care for their sick sons and daughters, never give up hoping that they too can successfully cope with the stresses, depression and stigmas that are caused by mental illness.

This book provides evidence from a single mom that there is a better, brighter tomorrow as long as she keeps her hope, not tire out, not give up, not give in and not give out.

## My Son's Heartbreaking Diagnosis

It another beautiful spring evening in Southern California was coming to its close. That beautiful day would turn into the worst day of my life. Unexpectedly, I was about to embark on a long, heart-breaking journey into the unknown that would forever change my life.

It was now a little past midnight. I was sleeping in my downstairs bedroom. My four children, three daughters and one son were all asleep in their rooms upstairs. That night, when my son came into my room, and sat on the edge of my bed, I was fast asleep. As soon as I saw him, I immediately got up and I knew something was wrong.

I got up as quickly as I could and sat next to him because I could clearly see he was in distress. At first, he was quiet, but distracted. I started to panic, but I tried hard to stay calm. I realized that my greatest fears were coming true.

While I reached out and held his hand, I asked him what was wrong. He was looking very frightened and told me he could not fall asleep. He then said to me, *"Mom, I don't know what is happening to me, something is wrong. I feel like a baby."* I felt

7

my heart stop beating. I became very distressed. I asked him if he would like to go to the emergency room. I knew I had to do something. I must quickly get him to a doctor. But, of course, like the countless times before, he refused.

I stayed up trying to comfort him the best that I could. I told him that I loved him. I tried to give him hope by telling him he would be ok in the morning. He went back upstairs to his bedroom, and I fell back to sleep. Although for the past couple of years, there were many subtle warning signs that a serious mental breakdown was imminent, I didn't realize that, on this night, his life had taken a dramatic turn.

It was now morning and I immediately got out of bed to check on my son. He was still awake, and pacing around in the house. He appeared very disconnected, something was very wrong with him. He was not hearing anything that I was saying. He was clearly distracted. I knew that he needed urgent medical attention. I became very nervous.

Again, I tried to take him to the hospital, but I could not convince him to go. He resisted my attempts to maneuver him into my car. At that time, the thought of dialing 911 did not occur to me. I simply kept comforting him. Later in time, I realized that I had made a serious mistake by not dialing 911.

*I made one of the greatest mistakes of my life!*

Instead of dialing 911 for help, I foolishly went to work that morning to ask for time off to take care of my son. At that time, I was very much afraid of losing my job because I was the sole provider. I had no idea that a drama was unfolding and the worst was yet to come.

One may ask, **"How could I make such a foolish decision?"**

The answer is *"I was afraid of losing my job."*

## My Son's Heartbreaking Prognosis

As I sat grief stricken and weeping in the doctor's office, my mind reflected on the time when my son was a healthy baby boy, who grew up to be a fine 18-year-old young man. He loved life, loved the outdoors, loved sports and loved people. He was sweet, caring and kind to everyone. He was a son any parent would want to have. Now, he is behind cold, scary walls of insanity.

Frightened and alone, I needed comfort. I needed strength. No one was there to comfort me. I dreaded waiting for the psychiatrist, and dreaded the diagnosis even more. I knew it was not going to be good. I silently and repeatedly prayed.

*"GOD, PLEASE HEAR MY PRAYERS AGAIN. PLEASE GIVE ME STRENGTH AND WISDOM MORE THAN EVER."*

My heart ached and my spirit was low. I wanted to die to spare myself the pain. Minutes passed stretching into what seemed to be hours.

The doctor finally arrived, and sat at his desk. My mind raced to thoughts of hearing good news from the doctor, maybe my son could come home the next day. To my greatest dismay, the situation worsened.

I then heard two words from the doctor, *"Paranoid Schizophrenia."* I did not know what those words meant. All that I remember is that those words sounded awful. I dreaded them. I knew paranoid was not good, but I could not recall ever hearing the word schizophrenia. **"SCHIZO WHAT?"** I asked the doctor.

*That moment was one of the most agonizing moments of my life.*

## I FELT TOTALLY DEFEATED

Nothing in my life could have prepared me, or given me any comfort for this diagnosis. It was a severe blow to my family. I went home and wept until I had no more tears.

# My Daughter's Heartbreaking Diagnosis

My daughter has been enduring bipolar for 18 years now. During the months before her break down, I was still reeling from my son's first psychotic breakdown. I was also still dealing with many struggles and challenges at home as well as my own stresses. The years that led up to my daughter's breakdown, were tumultuous and very similar to my son's pre-psychotic experiences.

She too was depressed and isolated herself. She expressed anger and rage towards me. She had severe delusions of grandeur. For months, she was convinced that she was the image of a popular, **'TV soap opera actress.'** She even imitated her hairstyles. For my daughter, it was real. **For me it was painful.**

Although I could identify a few of my daughter's symptoms such as depression, isolation, and the extreme emotional mood swings, it was unthinkable that mental illness would strike another child, suddenly and viciously.

Although both the elementary and middle school years were manageable for her because she was a bright student, she too had a difficult and challenging time attending high school.

During her first year in high school, she began having severe headaches. At least, that was how she described them. I took her to the doctor. After a thorough examination, he could not find anything that was causing her headaches.

Previously, my daughter was fitted with braces and retainers. I took her back to the Orthodontist to determine whether that could be the cause of her headaches. The Orthodontist assured me that being fitted for or wearing braces and retainers would not have caused headaches.

In retrospect, the symptoms were not headaches; rather, my daughter was experiencing psychosis. (My son experienced periods of reoccurring severe vomiting). She became more erratic, irrational and filled with anger. Eventually, she could not cope with school. That led to me asking the school for help.

After the school psychologist met with my daughter, she told me that she could not find anything wrong with her. That was an absolute misdiagnosis! *My daughter was seriously ill*. At times, even trained professionals, such as school psychologists and Interns with years of

13

experience, cannot detect warning signs of mental illness.

### *This was the second time that trained professionals failed my children.*

Coping with this illness was difficult for her. She eventually dropped out of high school. She later enrolled in Alternative Education. That too overwhelmed her. I was devastated and heartbroken, again.

As the months slowly dragged by, she became more agitated, aggressive and reclusive. Her symptoms continued and worsened.

Shortly after the night of her psychotic episode, she began antipsychotic treatments that prevented hospitalization. During this period, she tried taking a host of other medications. Although there were slight improvements, she suffered many side effects.

While taking the antipsychotic drug, Zyphrexia, she gained a massive amount of weight. She was less than100 pounds before taking the drug, and after taking this medication, she ballooned to almost 200 pounds within a 2-year period. She was extremely saddened by this and her emotional state worsened.

As time dragged on, she became more and more despondent about her weight. She asked her psychiatrist, on several occasions, to discontinue Zyphrexia. **The doctor refused and she kept taking it!**

To our greatest surprise, during one of her doctor's visits, the **psychiatrist told her to eat carrot sticks to lose the weight! We were shocked.** She never returned to that psychiatrist.

My daughter was very despondent on a daily basis. I comforted her as much as possible.

Soon after, I found another doctor that prescribed new medications that did not cause my daughter to gain weight, but she continued to struggle to find effective medications that would stabilize the bi-polar disorders.

After many years of struggles and relapses, excellent medications were prescribed and they are effectively controlling her illness.

It was my quick thinking getting her to the hospital, obtaining the proper medications and

15

the family's love and support that helped her through her horrible ordeals. She is now progressing well and experiencing success in her daily life.

Although there were many challenges for her to overcome during her recovery journey, she has risen to those challenges. She is continuing to progress well and finding real purpose in her life.

At only 16, bipolar was a harrowing experience for her as well as the entire family. It required every ounce of my love, patience, and understanding for helping her.

I had to come up with every practical ways that I knew possible to help her. I made sure she got a proper amount of rest, nutrition and exercise. I helped her with her medication but she knew the importance of taking them. I gave her one hundred percent support and gave her all the love that I could.

She had been struggling with feelings of low self-worth and low self-esteem and I gave her all the support in rebuilding her self-esteem. I never judge her or told her she was wrong or had the wrong attitude. I loved her. When she cried – I cried. When she laughed – I laughed with her.

16

The pain from bi-polar is real. Her pain was real. So I kept reassuring her that she will get well again.

The pain from bi-polar is real. Her pain was real. So I kept reassuring her that she will get well again.

My children had no control over their mental disorders, so I made sure that I never blamed them for anything they did because of their illnesses. Blaming a person because of mental illness is cruel. It makes them feel even more depressed.

Viewing bipolar as a serious sickness rather than a weakness will help us focus on how we can support our loved one.

During her depressed stage, she was more prone to thoughts of suicide. During her manic stage she lacked understand of what was perhaps wrong from right or the sudden change to irritation or rage towards me.

I cannot accurately describe the torment that comes from living with someone you love –

especially your children with bipolar. It is truly horrific.

It has been stated that bipolar may affect approximately 2 percent of the American population. There are 60 million others suffering globally. Many more may be undiagnosed, live on streets because or homelessness and unemployment, or no one to adequately care for them or support them – no one to love them.

Like schizophrenia, bipolar is very difficult to live with – there was no stability in our lives.

Like schizophrenia, bipolar was frightening and at times my children felt ashamed that they were ill with these horrible illnesses.

Like schizophrenia, my children cannot stop taking prescribed medications. Their brain chemistry must remain balance at all times.

Like schizophrenia, during her manic stages, my daughter's sleep pattern was severely disrupted.

Like schizophrenia, bipolar presented me with unique challenges that required me to find unique ways to coping.

18

Like schizophrenia, my daughter experienced many terrible lows followed by euphoric highs. Medications helped her but she still has daily struggles.

Today, there is good news. These illnesses are treatable. There are excellent doctors and medications available to help with day to day coping. Unfortunately, depending on where one lives, quality care is hard to find, and finding them is not always easy. Asking someone you know for help is ok to do.

## Major Depression and Stress

Since the inception of my children's illnesses 23 years ago, my life has changed drastically. Even with aggressive treatments, I could not predict with each day would present us, or what we would accomplishment each day, or the next day, or the next week. I had to be flexible and available at all times.

Suppose a psychiatrist told you that, your son or daughter was suffering with a devastating, incurable mental illness and may have only a one-third chance of recovery or that he may never recover?

Suppose that diagnosis and prognosis turned out to be accurate. How would you feel? How would you react? How would you cope?

**One day, unexpectedly, I had to face those very difficult and emotional questions, and it devastated me.**

Two decades ago when my son's prognosis was grim with only a one-third chance that he may recover or a one-third chance that he may remain in an unstable condition or a one-third chance that he may never recover, I was heartbroken, terrified and overwhelmed. It was physically and emotionally stressful to the point that it devastated me. It affected my every emotion.

I searched for help books and magazine articles. I went to the library and searched for family experiences of coping with schizophrenia. None gave me the comfort I desperately needed.

In my grief, I contacted the local National Alliance on Mental Illness (NAMI) for resources. They recommended that I attend group sessions at one of the local hospitals. I attended a few times, and some of the group sessions were helpful.

As mental illness rocked my world, and terror reigned over my family, it devastated us. The storminess of mental illness exhausted me, and my family fell to pieces. The most agonizing part of all was that it might never end. Yet, I set aside my anxieties and fears and courageously calmed my children's fears.

My children's illnesses did not present overnight; they suffered years of gradual break down. At times, the symptoms were frequent and severe. Other times, they were less severe and less frequent.

21

The most difficult period of this illness spanned a 16-year period: from 1991 to 2007. My family was in turmoil. For almost all of those years, my son refused to take his medication. And, for those 16 years, my family lived with doubts and fears. The challenges seemed insurmountable.

Mental illnesses took my son and daughter on a vicious emotional rollercoaster journey that was beyond my wildest imagination. Their journeys changed their lives in drastic ways. These journeys were long and arduous. Navigating them throughout those years was a trek during a dark, stormy, unending night.

During this period, I agonized because my adolescent son and daughter were not able to enjoy their teenage years and relationships or look forward to the joys of marriage and parenthood. Schizophrenia and bipolar robbed them of their happiness and joy of life.

The success that my children have had in overcoming their adversities has inspired me to share their story. When my son and daughter lost decades of their lives to mental illnesses, they became angry, fearful, isolated, and lost their abilities to make friends. I found ways to inspire them. I inspired them to keep fighting, keep hoping, keep focused and keep managing their illnesses.

The both have now rebuilt their self-worth, self-confidence and their personal growth has improved.

My encouragement definitely empowered them to succeed not only as individuals but to position themselves for success in life.

From a shocking diagnosis to a disheartening prognosis of practically no hope of recovery, their progress has encouraged me to write this book to promote mentally healthy lives – one person at a time – one family at a time - one community at a time, one city at a time. Hopefully, this will lead to a healthy nation – someday!

## Guilt

As a mother, my feelings of guilt were natural, but it was my biggest obstacle to overcome. I knew that I was not responsible for my son's paranoid schizophrenia or my daughter's bi-polar disorders. Yet, I continued to feel guilty, especially when I saw how desperately they were struggling to cope.

23

I felt guilty because I could not stop the illnesses or their relapses, sufferings and pain. I felt guilty each time my son relapsed and had to return to the psychiatric hospital, to the board and care facility or to a long-term care facility. I felt guilty when I left him in one of those places knowing how much he wanted to go home with me. I felt guilty when I became overwhelmed and, while frustrated, yelled at them.

In time, I felt slightly comforted knowing that my feelings of guilt were just a mere human reaction in times of tragedy.

## Grief

I felt compelled to grieve the loss of my son's and daughter's mental health. I realized that I needed to grieve before I could move forward. Once I completed my grieving, I was able to better care for them.

## Anger

I was angry and frustrated over the loss of my son's and daughter's educational and career opportunities, their social life and their work prospects, their personal achievements, and their academic deficiencies.

I was angry because of the discriminations and stigmas exhibited toward them. As time went on, I understood that anger was a symptom of my grief, and a natural response to the overwhelming magnitude of the demands being inflicted on me to help my son and daughter without the knowledge and resources that were necessary to quickly manage their loss of mental health. The more time passed, the more I understood that sadness, fears and anxieties manifested themselves as anger.

## Shame

I felt shame many times during this journey. At first, because I was unable to accept that both my children developed mental illnesses. In time, I learned that there were no reasons for me to feel ashamed.

## Blame

I blamed myself for not having knowledge about mental illness. I blamed myself for not getting quicker medical care for my son. I blamed myself for everything that went wrong.

## Fears

I had many fears. I experienced fears that my son would never recover per the 'LAW OF THIRDS.' I had fears of what would happen to my children if I die prematurely. I had fears that the police might shoot and kill my son, based on his previous encounters.

Over time, I learned to deal with my emotions and I looked beyond the illnesses towards the hope of a new day. I developed a positive attitude and thinking, which helped me to cope.

I learned how to work through these emotions, coped with them, and moved on with strength and courage.

Instead of finding an escape, as many do, I decided that I could not let mental illness; stigmas, stress and depression dominate my life.

Soon after, I immersed myself into finding new ways to cope. I developed an unwavering optimism to help my family with the many challenges that faced us.

As time went by, I began to develop and personalize my own coping skills, which gave me the comfort I desperately needed to manage my stress and get on with my life.

During this period, I struggled with many conflicting emotions and I had to find ways to work through them one by one. I wanted happiness and laughter in my home. Instead, there was chaos and anguish.

## Hope

My unwavering HOPE replaced my feelings of guilt, grief, anger, shame, blame and fear.

# Coping

As the daily stress from mental illness intensified, we lived from moment to moment, from day to day, never knowing when the situation within the family would suddenly change. There were times of immense tensions within the family.

My focus was very clear. It was to keep fighting for my son's and daughter's recovery from mental illnesses regardless of the cost to me. In order for me to accomplish my goal, I must endure to the end. If I failed, I would have lost my fight against mental illness. I was not willing for that to happen. With determination, I fought with all my strength to help my son and daughter cope with their illnesses. This was central for coping. I knew without a doubt that it would be difficult for me to do this. Regardless, I worked extremely hard to help them cope.

Successfully coping with all of this was near impossible.

My son's and daughter's coping and recovery rested solely on me. It was therefore necessary for me to find ways to help them cope as well as find ways for me to cope with my stresses and major depression.

All along the way, I prayed for success. However, as each day passed, it left them with cruel uncertainties of yet another day.

With each one of my emotions that robbed me of hope and comfort, I had to find new and different coping techniques.

My self-confidence was shattered. My self-worth plummeted to zero. At times, I felt that I just could not go on any longer. Crawling into bed and staying there seemed easier than searching for ways to cope.

Finding effective ways to cope with my son's and daughter's illnesses and my own stresses, depression and stigmas was not always easy. Finding new and effective ways to cope took endurance and discipline. I had to find personalized ways that worked for me.

During my search to find ways to cope, I was optimistic and determined to identify positive options.

Although I struggled to cope with a magnitude of unusual challenges, I worked tirelessly to overcome them. I coped with those struggles because I believed that I could. I drew strength, hope and comfort from scriptures and those were the bedrock of my ability to cope with my children's mental illnesses.

My success in coping with adversities was dependent on the effort that I put forth in finding ways that would really make a difference in my success.

I struggled with many conflicting emotions. There were many difficult days but I worked hard to overcome them. I fell down along the way, but staying down was not an option. Each time I got up and kept looking for new ways to cope.

Today, I continue to look for new ways to give comfort to others who are suffering, because I learned how to be sensitive to other people's sufferings.

My ability to help others was truly a blessing and a wonderful gift. It helped me to more effectively cope with my son's and daughter's illnesses.

31

If I had failed in coping with my son's and daughter's illnesses, I would have failed to cope with my own health challenges and ultimate recovery. I was determined for that not to happen.

Overcoming these great challenges has given me the opportunity to grow. I viewed my challenges as opportunities to build my character and become a stronger more resilient woman and mother. Instead of dwelling on things I could not change, I focused on what I could change, and learned to dwell on the positive aspects of my life.

Overcoming my challenges from severe adversities made me a stronger, more caring person.

I take great comfort from God's word especially in time of my distresses. "A heart broken and crushed, O God, you will not despise~Psalm 51.17.

"He will deliver the poor one crying for help, also the afflicted one and whoever has no helper. He will feel sorry for the lowly one and the poor one, and the souls of the poor ones he will save~Psalm 72:12-13. What comfort this brought me!

# Simple Effective Ways That Helped With Coping

## (Not in Chronically Order)

1) **NO CURE**: I was devastated when I first learned that there was no cure for schizophrenia or bi-polar. Today there is still no cure but I was comforted that there were effective medicines that manage and stabilize the illnesses~Romans 7:24, Romans 5:12, Revelation 21:3-4.

2) **NOT MY FAULT**: I was comforted when I accepted the fact that my son's and daughter's illnesses were not my fault. They were not the results of anything that I had done wrong or from bad parenting~1Peter 1:24, Ecclesiastes 9:11.

3) **PRAYERS:** Prayers were the bedrock of my coping. They gave me comfort and a bright hope for the future~1Peter 5:7, Philippians 4:6-7, Psalm 102.17, Psalm 62:8.

4) **MEDICATION:** Mental illness is like any other physical illness. It was vitally important for us to take medications as prescribed by our doctors.

33

5)     **GRIEVED:** It was necessary for me to grieve the loss of my son's and daughter's mental health. Once my grieving was over, I was able to cope~Phillipians4:6-7.

6)     **EMOTIONS**: I experienced every emotion imaginable. I cried throughout my journeys. I experienced guild, anger, fears, regrets, blame, shame and sadness. These emotions were also a part of my grieving process and they opened the way to my being able to cope~Isaiah 53:4-7.

7)     **ROUTINE:** Coping was hard but I returned to my regular daily routine as soon as I was able.

8)     **ACCEPTANCE**: Accepting my loved ones mental illnesses, not as failures on their part but as limitations and lessons learned. I was able to cope when I accepted their limitations.

9)     **STRESS**: When I accepted stressors as challenges in my life and did not view them as barriers, I managed them effectively and I was able to cope with them~Hebrews 13:5.

34

10) **ADAPT**: It was important for me to adapt to the ever-changing health conditions of my son and daughter. I adapted to the changing tides of mental illnesses by refocusing on anything positive in my life.

11) **CARE**: Providing my son and daughter with the best possible care was important to my coping. I was by their side every step of the way and provided love, comfort and guidance~Psalm 41:3.

12) **CRISIS:** Over the course of the years, I endured countless crises. I tried not to be overly anxious. I remained calm because there were many important decisions that I had to make~Matthew 6:25-34.

13) **GOOD JUDGMENT**: I used sound judgment, and made quick and rational decisions that would provide long-term benefits.

14) **PROBLEMS:** I identified problems and came up with solutions to help manage relapses and deal with stigmas.

35

15)　　**FOCUS:** My focus and mission was to see my son and daughter enjoy life as much as possible. I focused on their good qualities and not on the illnesses.

16)　　**STRENGTH:** Over the course of this journey, many of my friends considered me a strong person. Despite all of my strength, I still could not cope with the stressors and depression. It was extremely difficult, but I **never gave up.**

17)　　**ONE STEP**: I knew I could only take one-step at a time. I learned how to slow down, step back, take deep breaths then move forward one-step at a time. When I tried to do any more than that, I was unsuccessful.

18)　　**ONE DAY AT A TIME:** By living one day at a time, with this as my routine, I developed a selfless attitude and maintained a positive outlook on life~Matthew 6:25, 34.

19)　　**DOCTOR'S ADVICE**: I encouraged my son and daughter to follow their doctors' instructions in order to control their symptoms.

20)     **CLEAR IDEA:** I developed a clear idea of the things that I could do or could not do, and the things that I could change and could not change.

21)     **LETTING GO:** In order to cope well, I had to let go of everything negative in my life~Psalm 102.

22)     **DISCOURAGEMENT:** We live in a world that is filled with discouragements, stigmas and disappointments, so surrounding myself with encouraging, positive friends and relatives was helpful~Ephesians 4:25-26.

23)     **ADJUSTMENTS:** Taking keen note of my son's and daughter's emotions and tried to adapt my approach accordingly. Their thoughts and feelings were extremely fragile, so it was important for me to adjust to their needs.

24)    **TACT:** Tactfulness with my son and daughter was a key factor in diffusing situations that allowed for coping.

25)    **RESPONSIBILITY:** Taking full responsibility and worked tirelessly to help my son and daughter to regain their health paid off in a big way.

26)    **ROADBLOCKS:** There were many, many roadblocks and challenges but I tackled and overcame ALL OF THEM. Realizing that I could succeed motivated me even more to continue trying.

27)    **SELF-PITY:** I could have sat around day after day wallowing in self-pity and felt practically useless because no sooner, did I enjoy a little calmness before there was another crisis lurking around the corner. However, each time that I began to sink into what seemed to be a deep, dark hole, I would immediately take steps to avoid those feelings of uselessness. I would first quickly change my mental attitude toward my life and toward the illnesses.

28) **SELF-WORTH:** At first, losing one's self-confidence and self-worth is easy, but as time went on, I learned how to use my skills and abilities to combat those negative feelings. I have now gained peace of mind, confidence and self-esteem. I immersed myself into everything other than the illness, such as focusing on others. I involved myself in activities that created positive results.

29) **POSITIVE**: Rather than emphasizing or dwelling on the negative aspects of my life, I learned to focus on the positive aspects~Psalm 72:7-8.

30) **NEGATIVE THOUGHTS:** I saw my life as **"one hell of a mess,"** but those negative thoughts were only temporary. Other times I wished for a "typical family environment," especially when I saw other parents together with their healthy children. I vowed and remained zealously optimistic that the happy life my children and I once enjoyed would return~Matthew 6:34.

31) **PERSEVERE**: Persistence is an extremely important key in finding ways to

cope~Matthew 6:33; Luke 11:9; Romans 12:12.

32)     **DETERMINED:** I was determined to fight mental illness no matter what the cost. I gave up my dreams and hopes to help my son and daughter~Revelation 21:3-4.

33)     **HOPELESSNESS:** I never gave in to hopelessness or despair, even though for years the situation seemed hopeless. It did not make sense for me to lose the joy in life over the things that I could not control~Psalm 36:9; Psalm 34:18.

34)     **PATIENCE:** Learning how to cultivate patience was challenging, I patiently cared for my son and daughter, until they were able to care for themselves and both are now living independent lives~John 3:16.

35)     **RESENTMENTS AND FORGIVENESS:** I did not harbor resentments toward all those who were unkind and stigmatized my son and daughter. Over time I forgave those who were unkind~Colossians 3:13.

40

36) **WORRY:** Recently, my friend and I were travelling on a country road when we saw a sign on a building that read, **"WHY PRAY WHEN YOU CAN WORRY."** We looked at each other, nodded our heads in agreement, then we both busted out laughing. **HOW TRUE ARE THOSE WORDS?** I could not change my circumstances, worrying about it did not help me. I learned not to worry about what has not yet happened.

37) **NOT LOOKING BACK:** During my journey, with all the obligations and responsibilities, I was overwhelmed to the point of collapsing. Still, I refused to give up, look back or go back. I kept my positive thinking and attitude foremost in my mind. When others would have perhaps found escape by turning to drugs, alcohol, promiscuity, or just give up on hope, I worked tirelessly to maintain a clear mind and clear vision of my situation.

38) **CHANGES:** I eliminated the sources of my stress by making positive changes, and taking positive actions to make those changes. For example, I cried each time my son was admitted to the psychiatric hospital

or went to live in a board and care facility. But those visits were necessary just to get some peace in the home. It was a wonderful feeling when I was able to make changes or stop doing the things that were causing me stress and not producing positive results. I created good, pleasant, up building, and positive situations in my life.

39)     **LIFE-STYLE CHANGES**: Making small changes to my lifestyle as well as to my children's lifestyles helped with coping. Some were little changes, such as walking on the beach together or walking down Main Street eating hot, white chocolate chip cookies or ice cream. Other times, I made major changes such as brief stays with friends or relatives.

40)     **EXPECTATIONS:** Avoiding setting expectations that were too high for daily life assisted with coping.

41)     **BUDGET:** Setting a realistic budget is crucial. Learning to distinguish my family's needs from wants is a key to coping. Itemized the things we really needed, cut down on unnecessary purchases, and

42

refrained from making expensive purchases helped.

42) **SHOPPING**: Low cost nourishing foods was another key to my survival. Looked for small affordable gift items to give to those in need~Acts 20:35.

43) **EMOTIONS:** By expressing my emotions in many different ways, helped my children to learn that was ok to show emotions~Psalm 40:17.

44) **SADNESS:** I wrote what I was feeling when I felt sad or lonely~Psalm 34:18.

45) **CONVERSATIONS:** Begin conversations with strangers who would listen and whose comments are positive and encouraging.

46) **INSPIRED:** Reading about successful coping strategies they inspired me to focus on developing my coping skills.

47) **BALANCE:** Finding a balance in caring for my son and daughter is vitally important~Ecclesiastes 4:6.

48) **GOALS:** I accomplished goals in a timely manner~Ecclesiastes 12:1 and Proverbs 3:5-6.

49) **TOLERANT:** Being tolerant of other people's disabilities and failures made it easier to cope~Proverbs 15:1.

50) **OPTIMISTIC VIEW**: I developed an optimistic view of life. I pictured my children as healthy adults enjoying their lives. I learned not look back at the past. I learned not to dwell on, **'what might have been.'** I learned to focus on the good things in life~Luke 21:28-31.

51) **VISUALIZE**: Visualization worked well. My goals of seeing my children well again was my priority and I believed them to be real and that they would come true. Then I hoped for success~Proverbs 22:3.

52) **REALISTIC VIEW**: I developed a realistic view of my son's and daughter's illnesses. I viewed each situation as challenges to overcome instead of disasters. Therefore, I was able to put into

44

practice the advice I received from one of my friends, **"Enjoy the good days and do not worry about the difficult ones."**

53)    **CHARACTER**: I assisted my son and daughter to develop real strength of character helped with my coping.

54)    **READ**: It was important for me to read, occasionally only a few lines a day  but I kept on reading and never gave up~Romans 7:22, Joshua 1:8, Psalm 1:2.

55)    **MEDITATE**: Meditation helped me to remain positive~Psalm 1:2 and Psalm 119:97.

56)    **NUTRITION**: Nutritious foods, lots of water and plenty of sleep, helped me to cope~Proverbs 23:20, Matthew 9:12.

57)    **VISITS**: I spent weekends visiting friends and relatives and occasionally stayed overnight.

58)    **REST**: I parked in shopping centers and slept for an hour or two just to get a

break from the stressors at home~Ecclesiastes 4:6.

59)     **LIVE ONE DAY AT A TIME**: I learned to live one day at a time. Looking beyond this was overwhelming, counterproductive and stressful.

60)     **COMMUNICATE**: I encouraged all my children to communicate with each other especially because we were adapting to great challenges.

61)     **LISTEN**: I encouraged all my children to listen to each other, and help each other. Even though it was extremely difficult for all my children to talk about our family tragedies, I encouraged them to talk about it.

62)     **FEELINGS**: I learned to accept my children's concerns and feelings about mental illness. I listened to each of my children with compassion, as it was vitally important to their emotional wellness. I gave each of them advice to fit their individual needs.

46

63)    **SUCCESS STORIES**: My children and I made conscious efforts to make time to listen to the success stories of others, or read about their successes. Over time, I found that taking time to listen and read about other people's adversities helped me to cope with my problems, by momentarily diminishing their weight. I read real life success stories such as the one about the courageous mother whose two children had leukemia, or the strength of a woman with cancer who endured a double mastectomy. I read many blogs about people having schizophrenia and bi-polar illnesses lived productive lives.

64)    **LIMITATIONS**: I knew my limitations. I knew what I could do and what I could not accomplish. I learned how to recognize my limitations in caring for my son and daughter. I learned to recognize my children's limitations and accepted them~1Corinthians 15:58, 1 Kings 19:5-7.

65)    **DENIAL**: I quickly discovered the value of staying away from anyone who is in denial of mental illnesses or taking

psychiatric medications. Their negative attitudes drained my energy.

66)     **HARSH WORDS**: Harsh words are destructive. I avoided harsh words that were hurtful to others or to me~Matthew 5:23-25.

67)     **CONFLICTS**: Conflicts and arguments primarily do not accomplish anything worthwhile so I avoided conflicts~Proverbs 19:11.

68)     **CRY**: There were countless times when I sat alone in the dark of night and cried. Other times I would get up in the wee hours of the mornings, sat alone in my living room and weep while my children slept upstairs.

69)     **BLESSINGS**: I coped by counting my blessings, no matter how small they were.

70)     **FUN**: I did fun things that brought joy and happiness into my life.

48

71)   **WHY NOT ME?** Over the course of time, I learned to ask, **"Why not me?,"** instead of, **"Why me?"**

72)   **INSPIRATION:** I provided my son and daughter with tools that would motivate and inspire them. I coped well when they made progress.

73)   **RECOVERY:** To cope, I focused my attention on my son's and daughter's recovery process.

74)   **CONFIDENCE:** It was of paramount importance to me to have full confidence in my children's abilities to recover.

75)   **STRENGTHS:** I differentiate my strengths from my weaknesses as well as those of my children.

76)   **NEVER GIVING UP:** I never 'gave up hope.' If I had given up hoping, I would have failed my children.

77)   **TIMEFRAME:** Allowing my son and daughter to cope at their own pace and in their own time helped me.

49

78)     **FRIENDS:** I did not allow negative comments from friends to discourage me~Proverbs 17:17.

79)     **RELATIVES:** Negative words hurt. I did not allow negative comments from relatives to discourage me.

80)     **JUDGE:** I reached out to relatives and friends who were kind and caring.

81)     **SKILLS:** At nights when I could not sleep, I would practice typing to increase my speed.

**82)     HUMOR**: Humor played an important role in my ability to cope. *"Humor is a universal coping mechanism when faced with all varieties of stress, states Dr. Reiss." The Vancouver Sun.*

83)     **LAUGHTER**: Laughter was therapy for me, and it is still extremely successful in my coping~1 Timothy 1:11; Ecclesiastes 1:4.

84)     **SMILE:** I smiled even when I did not feel like smiling.

85)     **TALKING**: Talking about my son's and daughter's illnesses helped me to cope.

86)     **CLEAR VISION**: Maintaining a clear vision of a positive outcome for my children's futures was one of my priorities.

87)     **FOCUSED**: I focused on my son's and daughter's happiness instead of their illnesses.

88)     **SET GOALS**: Setting small, achievable, personal goals for myself and for my son and daughter helped me~Philippians 1:10.

89)     **AFFIRMATIONS**: Affirmations helped me cope. **"I can do it." "I must cope." "I must believe that I will cope."**

90)     **SELF-CONFIDENCE:** I coped well when I had confidence in my ability to care for my son and daughter and see them progressed to health.

51

91)     **FAITH:** My experience along with my faith has helped me to live a purposeful life.

92)     **APPRECIATION**:                    Showing appreciation for life was important for me. I worked hard to maintain my appreciation no matter how small it felt.

93)     **NEVER LOOKED BACK**: If I had looked back, I would have stayed in the past. I wanted to move into the future.

94)     **ADDICTIONS**: I had no interest in any type of substance abuse or addictions. I coped by relying on a clear mind.

95)     **DREAM:** I encouraged my son and daughter to be positive. I taught them to dream, and never give up of their dreams.

96)     **FUTURE**: Focusing on a bright future definitely helps so I encouraged my son and daughter to focus on their future. I taught them to love themselves, live life and love people. I taught them how to be kind compassionate and caring to all.

97)    **UNIQUE:** I constantly reminded my son and daughter that they are unique, important and special.

98)    **SCRIPTURES**: My spiritual life was foremost in my life so I searched the scriptures daily for verses that comforted me. "Read God's word daily~Psalm 63:6.

99)    **WORKING WITH MY SON AND DAUGHTER**: I encouraged my son and daughter to accept their illnesses. I encouraged them to accept the things that they cannot change and change only the things that they could change. I encouraged them to be strong and courageous.

100)    **HOPE**: Without hope, there is no future. I never gave up hope of coping and recovery and I never lost hope. I kept my hope alive by looking ahead to a bright future.

101)    Inspiring my son and daughter to think, read, study and progress was crucial

to their futures. I prepared them with skills that would make them successful.

102)    I urged my son and daughter to develop their self-worth, and self-confidence to overcome barriers of stigmas and discriminations.

103)    Reassuring my son and daughter to set small, attainable goals would help them become productive. I helped them to accomplish those goals.

104)    **VOLUNTEER WORK:** I provided transportation for the elderly and the disabled~Acts 20:35.

105)    Supporting other in their struggles, I conducted Computer-training and Job Readiness classes at a Woman's shelter.

106)    I inspired young boys to build typing skills by conducting computer-keyboarding classes at a Boys Club.

107)    I volunteered and conducted Job Readiness Interviewing skills at Goodwill Industries.

108) I held a weekly bible study group setting with the elderly and the disabled at a group home.

109) I actively participated in door-to-door community services by providing practical spiritual instructions for daily living.

110) Visiting sick friends at nursing homes was therapeutic for me.

111) I visited board and care facilities and gave residents little personal gift items. I would also take them fruits, candies, cookies and clothing.

112) I took friends shopping at Wal-Mart then stopped in at McDonald's or Burger King for hamburgers and fries.

113) I offered kind, sincere words of praise to others.

114) When I asked someone, **"How are you today?"** I really meant it. I listened to them and gave encouragement.

115)   I learned to treat the mentally ill person with respect and dignity and offered assistance whenever it was within my means.

116)   My son and daughter enjoyed frequent long walks and breathing fresh air.

117)   My son and daughter loved walking in the sunshine. We suntanned to a golden brown along with our daily exercise.

118)   We enjoyed the fragrant aromas and the dramatic beauty of the flowers and blooming trees.

119)   Strolling around town on cool breezy days was refreshing.

120)   Talking walks under beautiful moonlit skies and bright starry nights were very calming.

121)   We watched and fed the birds, which filled us with feelings of freedom.

122)   We walked on many nature trails and enjoyed the openness of the outdoors.

123) My children and I strolled around ponds and fed ducks.

124) My family and I spent countless days relaxing in beautiful parks, enjoyed delicious picnic lunches and ate fresh berries and ripe watermelons.

125) My children and I relaxed in the lush, green grass, sometimes we read the bible. Other times we just meditated.

126) My son and I spent countless hours playing tennis and basketball.

127) My son and I spent many hours walking on sandy beaches and enjoying the cool ocean breeze. We watched the elegant surfers, and at times searched for unusual seashells.

128) My family and I enjoyed many picnic lunches and many bon fires on cool nights. We ate marshmallows straight from the fire pits. We enjoyed sharing our food with the birds that always seemed hungry.

129)     I enjoyed hiking up the trails that led to many wonderful waterfalls and relaxed in the cool, refreshing waters of the Blue Ridge Mountains in Western North Carolina.

130)     My son and I took leisurely, daily walks to the local library and read many books that really interested us.

131)     We enjoyed many relaxing walks on downtown Main Street, ate ice cream cones and enjoyed delicious pastries.

132)     Walked and window-shopped at local malls and enjoyed eating an egg roll or two.

133)     Listened to calming music such as beautiful religious melodies. We enjoyed listening to a wide variety of tranquility music.

134)     We swam at the community pool, lounged under the sun and enjoyed picnic lunches. Other times we just relaxed in the Jacuzzi.

135) Exercise was important to us; we frequently worked out at the gym.

136) On weekends, we enjoyed friendly, home-based and park gatherings.

137) We frequently enjoyed watching old movies.

138) My daughter and I especially enjoyed massages and chiropractic treatments. Both helped to reduce our emotional pain and stress.

139) My daughter and I spent countless hours in Lowe and Home Depot home gardening stores. We loved gardening. During the summer, we spent countless hours mowing the lawn and planted beautiful flowers.

140) Many times, my son and I relaxed at fast food eateries such as Arby's, McDonalds, Burger King, Kentucky Fried Chicken, and we especially enjoyed Long John Silver from time to time. Since we were on a tight budget, we took advantage of buy-one get-one free coupons from

mailings and occasionally from the back of grocery store receipts. These were fun times that afforded us the opportunity to strengthen our relationship and build stronger bonds with each other.

141) Continuous reinforcement of our family bonds by spending as much time as possible enjoying each other and developing their skills for the workforce.

# Conclusion

The World Health Organization stated, "Globally, more than 400 million people suffer from depression. Many millions more have some mental problems."

As the outlook for mental illness continues to rest on the hope of finding a cure, the reality of seeing that outcome was of paramount importance to me. Medical treatments have dramatically improved since my son and daughter first became ill over two decades ago, but according to many experts, research indicates that any cure is still in the embryonic stages.

Based on this, I sacrificed my personal pursuits and worked tirelessly to help my son and daughter to find ways to cope, and move on to the next stages of their lives. Today, they are both living independent lives.

Families, especially single moms with mentally ill sons and daughters are struggling to cope because of the vast amount of challenges associated with these illnesses.

It takes courage, perseverance and strength to cope. It takes not giving up or giving out. It takes fighting until you win the fight against mental illness.

After the pain my family suffered because of stigmas, I taught those young children how vitally important it is to show more empathy and sensitivity to the mentally ill; to treat those who are ill the way my nieces and nephews would like to be treated if they were ill – mentally or otherwise. When anyone showed kindness to my children, we really appreciated them.

I FIRMLY BELIEVE THAT IT IS ONE'S MORAL OBLIGATION AND, FOR THOSE OF US WHO ARE CHRISTIANS, IT IS OUR CHRIST LIKE DUTY TO SHOW EMPATHY TO EVERYONE.

Rebuilding and reintegrating into a society that stigmatizes is very difficult and has been impossible for too many Americans. It requires understanding, kindness, support and empathy from every source and sector of society, but especially from loved ones. It requires patience, training and education from all, and by all. Americans who are suffering with this type of illness need help in general as well as kindness, and compassion, no matter how small it may be.

Although the mental health sector is significantly progressing in its efforts to educate the public about stigmas, until there is a cure for mental illnesses, stigmas may become permanently interwoven into the fabric of America if Americans allow it to happen. To ensure that this does not become the norm, de-stigmatizing mental illness requires the input of all Americans one individual at a time, one family at a time, one organization at a time and one community at a time.

Those living and suffering with mental illnesses face numerous challenges on a daily basis. There are many hardships and anxieties to overcome. Lives are shattered, homes are broken, marriages and relationships sometimes fail. Many faced lack of social and personal skills, lack of education, job training and job skills. All these may lead one to homelessness, economic hardships and into poverty.

If mental illness is undiagnosed, left untreated, or if not treated in a timely manner with effective medications and therapies then the frightening realities of life becomes a true disaster.

Coping is difficult. Accessing the road to recovery is even harder. Today, the mental health sector is making significant progress in raising awareness

63

about early diagnosis and treatment options. Although there is no cure, one can learn to live a productive life despite mental illness.

Rebuilding and reintegrating in society is not easy. It requires love, support and empathy from every source and sector of society, but especially from loved ones. It requires patience, re-training and education.

As the number of people who show empathy toward the mentally ill increases, bridging the gap on making progress in their lives, and in the workplace also increases.

As the outlook for mental illness continues to rest on the hope of finding a cure, the reality of seeing the recovery outcome of my son and daughter is of paramount importance to me.

During my years of struggles, I examined my life for all the things that brought me happiness. Examining my own life helped me to understand other people's struggles and hardships and I looked for ways in which I could help them.

I then developed a positive mind-set to treat others with dignity and respect regardless of their

64

disabilities or adversities, or what difficulties they were experiencing.

As I reflect on my life, I am most grateful to have had the faith and trust in God that helped me cope with these incurable mental illnesses. During the periods of unbearable grief, I prayed to God incessantly and fervently. My heart is filled with gratitude from the comfort I absorbed from scriptures. Although the bible is not a medical guidebook, reading it regularly helped me cope with the struggles of dealing with mental illness.

## Quotations

**The National Mental Health Association** stated, *"Mental health problems affect one in every five young people at any given time. An estimated two-thirds of all young people with mental health problems are not receiving the help they need."* The article further states, *"Suicide is the third leading cause of death for 15- to 24-years-olds and the sixth leading cause of death for 5- to 15-year-olds."*

**World Health Organization** issued a Release stating, *"There are over 80 million people around the world with severe mental disorders, such as schizophrenia and bipolar affective disorder (manic depressive illness). In addition, 400 million people suffer from depression."*

**According to Dr. Cheryl Lane, PhD.** www.schizophrenia.com, *"Attempting to find new work after a diagnosis of schizophrenia can be particularly difficult. If a potential employer is aware of the person's diagnosis, discrimination may hinder landing a job. Also, significant stigma is associated with any major mental illness."*

Dr. Lane further states, *"A possible solution for many individuals is to become involved in some sort of vocational training or rehabilitation program. They can learn new skills and get help with learning or improving social skills. These programs can also help them function more fully and develop better thinking skills. Additionally, working with a psychotherapist can help with self-esteem issues, stress management and making the best choices in terms of whether to work."*

**Columbia University's Department of Psychiatry stated that** *"To understand and promote recovery from serious mental illnesses, it is important to study the perspectives of individuals who are coping with mental health problems. The aim of the present study was to examine identity-related themes in published self-narratives of family members and individuals with serious mental illness. It adds to the body of research addressing how identity affects the process of recovery and identifies potential opportunities for using published narratives to support individuals as they move toward positive identities that facilitate recovery."*

**The National Institute of Mental Health (NIMH),** stated, *"Schizophrenia is a chronic, severe, and disabling brain disorder that has affected people throughout history. About 1 percent of Americans have the disease."*

**World Fellowship for Schizophrenia and Allied Disorders,** states, *"Schizophrenia is the most persistent and disabling of the major mental illness...While it is treatable in many cases there is yet no cure..."*

**A psychiatrist, as recorded in a medical journal** [16 (2) 2003], was quoted as saying, *"It is well known that schizophrenia is a chronic, generally life-long, mental illness that significantly debilitates afflicted individuals and severely compromises their function and quality of life."*

**The Nutritional Management of Schizophrenia** described schizophrenia in this way, *"Schizophrenia may be caused by genetic predisposing factors or environmental influences."*

**University of Alberta Press Release,** stated, *"Schizophrenia is a biochemical brain disorder characterized by delusions, disordered, thinking, hallucinations and a lack of motivation and energy."*

**U.S. National Institutes on Mental Health (NIMH)** stated, *"1.1 percent of the U.S. population age 18 and older in any given year."* The article goes on to state, *"Scientists have long known that Schizophrenia runs in families, it occurs in 10% of* *people who have first-degree relatives with the disorder." Additionally, it stated, "Many people with Schizophrenia improve enough to lead independent, satisfying lives."*

**National Alliance on Mental Illness** stated, *"Schizophrenia is a serious mental illness that affects 2.4 million American adults over the age of 18."*

**The American Psychiatric Association** stated regarding one possible cause of Schizophrenia, *"Although the origin of Schizophrenia has not been identified, Scientists know that there are some hereditary or genetic predispositions for the disease because it runs in families."*

**American Psychiatric Association,** Jeffrey Draine, Ph.D. and several or his colleagues wrote an article stated, *"With an improved understanding of the disease and effective therapies, those with schizophrenia can have a full life, hold a job, and live in the community or with their family."*

**World Health Organization** stated, *"More than 90% of all cases of suicide are associated with mental disorders such as depression, schizophrenia, and alcoholism,"* notes Dr.

69

Benedetto Saraceno, Director of the Department of Mental Health for WHO, October 9, 2006.

**The National Advisory Mental Health Council of the WHO stated**, *"Schizophrenia is a (mental) disorder associated with high levels of social burden and cost, as well as an incalculable amount of individual pain and suffering."*

**World Health Organization,** *i*n a 1992 article, *quoted Leete as saying, "Stigma is shameful and displays a shameful part in human behavior. Stigma is damaging and destructive, it is a multi-layered and complex problem."*

***WHO published an article by Deegan*** *in 1980. The article stated, "Stigmas act as a powerful barrier to treatment not because of the fear of being labeled as mentally ill, but because too often mental health professionals and mental health services as a whole, often in a subtle way display negative or rejecting attitudes towards users and perpetuate practices fostering segregation, dependency and powerlessness.*

**The Queensland Alliance** for Mental Health observed, "P*eople with mental health problems are "frequently the object of ridicule or derision and are depicted within the media as being* *violent, impulsive and incompetent." It also found that the myth surrounding violence has not been dispelled, despite evidence to the contrary.*

**Mental Illness Policy** stated, *"Americans with untreated schizophrenia and manic-depressive illness comprise one-third or 250,000, of the estimated 744,000 homeless population." The quality of life for these individuals is abysmal. Many are victimized regularly.* (mentalillnesspolicy.org)

Nations for Mental Health, Schizophrenia and Public Health, Division of Mental Health, Chapter 4, Consequences of Schizophrenia, Health, National Advisory Mental Health Council, World Health Organization, (WHO) (Leete 1982) stated, *"Stigma represents a major challenge with regard to the integration of persons with schizophrenia...into the community."* The article further states, "There are over 350 million people globally of all ages suffering from depression."

"Exposure to trauma and stress at a young age can cause mental disorders. Genetics, nutrition, perinatal infections and exposure to environmental hazards are also factors," stated the World Health Organization, 2014.

## *What Is Schizophrenia*

No matter how schizophrenia is defined, it is impossible to explain the full magnitude of the destructiveness of this illness.

According to the Encarta Dictionary, *"schiz-o— phre-ni-a, is 'a severe psychiatric disorder with symptoms of emotional instability, detachment from reality, and withdrawal into the self.'"*

According to the National Institute of Mental Health (NIMH), *"Schizophrenia is a chronic, severe and disabling brain disorder that has affected people throughout history."* About 1% of Americans have the disease. Specifically, 1.1 percent of Americans who are 18 and older are affected in any given year. The article goes on to state, *"Scientists have long known that Schizophrenia runs in families ... it occurs in 10% of people who have first-degree relatives with the disorder."*

According to the World Fellowship for Schizophrenia and Allied Disorders, *"Schizophrenia is the most persistent and disabling of the major mental illnesses...While it is treatable in many cases, there is yet no cure..."*

A Medical Journal, Current. Opin. Psychiatry 16 (2) 2003 contained the quote, *"It is well known that schizophrenia is a chronic, generally life-long, mental illness that significantly debilitates afflicted individuals and severely compromises their function and quality of life."*

The Nutritional Management of Schizophrenia described it in this way, *"Schizophrenia may be caused by genetic predisposing factors or environmental influences."*

University of Alberta Press Release, states, *"Schizophrenia is a biochemical brain disorder characterized by delusions, disordered thinking, hallucinations and a lack of motivation and energy."*

William Carpenter, Director of the Maryland Psychiatric Research Center stated, *"It's a terrible disease and major public health problems."*

Daniel Weinberger of the NIMH stated, *"Whatever the anatomical change in schizophrenia, it's a very small one. This is not a stroke. This is not a massive failure of brain development - this is a subtle, subtle defect."*

According to the World Health Organization, (WHO), Media Centre dated June 2007, Geneva, *"There are nearly 54 million people around the world with severe mental disorders, such as schizophrenia and bipolar affective disorder (manic depressive illness). In addition, 154 million people suffer from depression."*

National Alliance on Mental Illness. (NAMI) stated, *"Schizophrenia is a serious mental illness that affects 2.4 million American adults over the age of 18."*

Regarding one possible cause of Schizophrenia, the American Psychiatric Association is convinced that, *"Although the origin of Schizophrenia has not been identified, Scientists know that there are...hereditary or genetic predispositions for the disease because it runs in families."*

If these reports are correct, Schizophrenia may strike anyone at any time. It has no barriers, no boundaries no ethnic demarcations and it does not discriminate. It strikes those in every class, in every occupation, the young and old, man and woman, rich and poor, blacks, whites, browns, and all other colors. It strikes the educated and the illiterate, the powerful and the famous as well as movie stars, those with prestige and those who have achieved in every field. It does not discriminate based on religious affiliation, cultural background or economic status.

Since it strikes anyone at any time, it could be: a spouse, a father or mother, a son or daughter, aunts or uncles, nieces or nephews, cousins, friends, neighbors, workmates, school mates, acquaintances or YOU.

*It has been said that, 'knowledge is power.' Knowledge saves lives from the bitter effects of mental illness.*

In reality, no scientific research has resulted in findings to support a possible cure. Based on this fact, for decades my son's outcome appeared grim. However, thanks to modern, effective and available medicines the intensity and frequency of the illness are manageable. While the illness continues to cause minor impairments in function despite treatments and family support, my family and I successfully live with this illness.

If mental illness is untreated, or if not treated in a timely manner, the frightening reality of suicide is a possibility. The quicker one begins the right treatment program, the better the chance of recovery will be.

The cause of Schizophrenia is still unknown. Fortunately, for the estimated 10% of the

American population, and their families as well as friends and communities, who are affected by this illness, many excellent anti-psychotic medications are currently available.

Schizophrenia is a mental illness that causes unusual thinking and feelings. Many people who have this illness experience auditory hallucinations, psychosis and delusions on an ongoing basis.

Psychosis is a *"psychiatric disorder that is marked by delusions, hallucinations, incoherence, and distorted perceptions of reality,"* states the Encyclopedia Britannica.

*"Delusions are false beliefs that are not part of the person's culture and do not change. The person believes delusions even after other people prove that the beliefs are not true or logical,"* states the National Institute of Mental Health (NIMH), March 2012.

## What is bipolar

"Bipolar disorder also known as manic-depressive disorder is a condition characterized by depressive episodes interspersed with periods of which mood and energy are excessively elevated well beyond normal levels of a good mood," stated Barbara D. Ingersoll and Sam Goldstein.

Bipolar affective disorder – This disorder affects about 60 million people worldwide.  It typically consists of both manic and depressive episodes separated by periods of normal mood. Manic episodes involve elevated or irritable mood, over-activity, …. Decreased need for sleep, inflated self-esteem," stated the World Health Organization 2014.

**Social Psychiatry and Psychiatric**, in a 1994 study stated, *"Women with schizophrenia and bi-polar disorders are more likely to be raped multiple times."*

The National Institute on Mental Health (NIMH) States:

**"Bipolar disorder**, also called manic-depressive illness, is not as common as major depression or persistent depressive disorder. Bipolar disorder is characterized by cycling mood changes—from extreme highs (e.g., mania) to extreme lows …..")

**http://www.cdc.gov/mentalhealth/basics/ment al-illness/bipolar.htm**

77

# What is Depression

The National Institute on Mental Health (NIMH) states:

"Depression is a common but serious illness. Most who experience depression need treatment to get better ..."

http://www.nimh.nih.gov/health/index.shtml

www.samhsa.gov/

## *Some Symptoms of Depression*

PLEASE GO TO THE NATIONAL INSTITUTE ON MENTAL HEALTH WEBSITE AT http://www.nimh.nih.gov/health/publications/de pression/index.shtml

Depression or depressive disorders, is a leading cause of disability in the United States as well as worldwide. It affects an estimated 9.5 percent of American adults in a given year. Nearly twice as many women as men have depression. Epidemiological studies have reported that up to 2.5 percent of children and 8.3 percent of adolescents in the United States suffer from depression.

"Depression affects 400 million globally," stated WHO 2014.

# Resources

## Depression and Bipolar Support Alliance (DBSA)
730 N. Franklin Street, Suite 501
Chicago, IL 60610-7204
Phone Number: (312) 642-0049
Toll-Free Number: (800) 826-3632
Fax Number: (312) 642-7243
www.dbsalliance.org

## American Psychiatric Association
1000 Wilson Blvd, Suite 1825
Arlington, VA 22209-3901
Phone Number: (703) 907-7300
Email Address: apa@psych.org
www.psych.org

## National Institute of Mental Health
http://www.nimh.nih.gov/health/publications/de
pression/index.shtml

## Centers for Disease Control and Prevention
http://www.cdc.gov/mentalhealth/basics/mental-
illness.htm

http://www.cdc.gov/mentalhealth/basics/mental-
illness/psychotic.htm

http://www.cdc.gov/mentalhealth/about_us/stigma-illness.htm

## Author

Alyse King is the mother of four courageous children, one wonderful son and three delightful daughters. She is also a grandmother of one beautiful granddaughter and four adorable grandsons.

For over two decades, Ms. King has tirelessly focused her attention on caring for two of her four children who had been struggling with chronic illnesses since they were teenagers. She has successfully helped them cope with their illnesses and reintegrate into society by retraining them to live independently and become financially self-reliant, provided them with the soft skills training that are vitally important to self-improvement and skills for the job market.

Ms. King's happiness about her ability to help her son and daughter has encouraged her to share the "recovery techniques" she used. She self-published seven books titled, "A Letter to Schizophrenia from a Mother," "When Schizophrenia Strikes," "When Bi-Polar Strikes," "140 Ways Coping with Depression," "Schizophrenia, Bi-Polar, Stress and Stigmas," "Finding Hope in a Hopeless World," and a self-help Workbook titled, "Day After Day Coping with Mental Illness - Support for Individuals and Families."

These books tell how she rebuilt her children's lives by helping them with skills that are necessary for coping, managing daily in-home routines, adhering to medical reminders, as well as the increasing joy she felt after each hurdle that marked their movement beyond illness.

The experiences gained as the mother of children who are successfully recovering from mental illnesses, as well as being their full time caregiver, instructor and re-trainer, has enabled her to accumulate many years of expertise. Additionally, her prior experience as a trainer in the private sector has added necessary, unique tools for writing these books.

Alyse King also self-published three Self-Help Guides titled, "Reintegrating after Traumatic Life Experience for: "Self Improvement," "Job Preparation," and "How to Keep Your Job." The

Workbooks provide continuing education and training for returning to employment or becoming financially independent. The Workbooks share the systematic techniques that Ms. King used in helping her children to develop personal skills and skills for hunting for a job, securing the job and holding the job.

She also self-published, "A Trainers' Manual for "Self-Improvement, Job Preparation, Job Retention." The Trainers' Manual provides guidance to all who wish to develop programs to help others to find work or achieve financial independence.

Alyse also self-published, "Comfort and Hope – Death- Reflections from Scriptures," and three non-fiction titles, "A 30-Day Online Romance, Based on a True Story - Part 1," "Confessions from A 30-Day Online Romance, Based on a True Story - Part 2, and "A Follow-Up of Confessions from A 30-Day Online Romance, Based on a True Story - Part 3."

Ms. King grew up and was educated on a beautiful Caribbean Island; married in her 20's and has been a homemaker, mother and sole provider for her family. Later, divorced, she relocated to Southern California with her four children.

The author currently resides in the beautiful Blue Ridge Mountains in Western North Carolina. Her son and youngest daughter also live in North Carolina. Her other two eldest daughters and all five grandchildren remain in Southern California. She frequently travels to California to visit her family and friends.

Ms. King's goal is to utilize her expertise in both the health and educational sectors. For the past several years, she has been working towards that goal by volunteering her time to help friends who are struggling to cope with mental illness.

Website: cmitrainingservices.com
E-mail: cmitrainingservices@gmail.com
http://www.amazon.com/-/e/B001KE71BQ
https://www.smashwords.com/books/search?query=alyse+king
http://www.linkedin.com/in/alyseking
https://www.facebook.com/alyse.king.12382

# Notes

88

# Notes

# Notes

www.ingramcontent.com/pod-product-compliance
Lightning Source LLC
Chambersburg PA
CBHW070749290526
45795CB00002B/543